CW00351149

The Big

BORIS

Compiled by
IAIN DALE

First published in Great Britain in 2011 by
Biteback Publishing Ltd
Westminster Tower
3 Albert Embankment
London
SE1 7SP
Copyright © Iain Dale 2011

Illustrations courtesy of Hoby, www.hobycartoons.com

This book is an updated version of *The Little Book of Boris*, published by Harriman House in 2007.

ISBN 978-1-84954-119-0

10 9 8 7 6 5 4 3 2 1

A CIP catalogue record for this book is available from the British Library.

Set in Sun Serif and Twentieth Century by Namkwan Cho
Cover design by Namkwan Cho

Printed and bound in Great Britain by
CPI Group (UK) Ltd, Croydon, CR0 4YY

The Bigger Book of Boris

FOREWORD

There are few politicians who could genuinely be described as a phenomenon. Boris Johnson is one. His appearances on *Have I Got News For You* propelled him into the political stratosphere, building him a fan base way beyond the confines of politics. Boris has star quality. He's loved by many, ridiculed by some, feared by others.

My abiding memory of Boris was spending a day with him when I was campaigning as the Conservative Party candidate in North Norfolk. Boris kindly agreed to come and support my efforts to be an MP (which sadly failed!). I had heard terrible stories of him being late or turning up on the wrong day, so when I answered the phone at ten to nine that morning, my heart was already in my mouth. I thought I'd covered every organisational base there was to cover but, oh no, I hadn't. 'Morning, old bean,' chirruped Boris. 'Nearly at the station now.' As the train was due to depart for Norwich at 9am, I was already worried. 'Where exactly are you, Boris?' I whimpered. 'Just coming into King's Cross now,' came the rather worrying response. Why worrying? Well, he was supposed to be at Liverpool Street. I just about managed not to cry, and rapidly created Plan B. I got him on the train to King's Lynn – a mere ninety-minute drive from my home near North Walsham, and then of course a ninety-minute drive back.

Bearing in mind he was due to speak at a lunch for 150 people at 1pm, things were not looking good. In the end we managed to go to the glass-making factory, do an interview with North Norfolk Radio and conduct an interview with the local paper in the back of the car without too much trouble. However, it meant we were forty-five minutes late for the lunch.

We walked into the room and I expected to be lynched. But they all stood and cheered, because frankly they had never expected him to be on time. 'Good old Boris,' they cried. Only Boris could have got away with it. Meanwhile, I slumped into my chair, a nervous wreck, thinking to myself, 'Never again.'

In 2008 he successfully ousted Ken Livingstone as Mayor of London. Since then he has brought a new energy and unique style of governance to City Hall. As an LBC radio presenter I have had the pleasure of interviewing Boris on a few occasions over the last year, and his charm and wit remain. He gives good interview, as they say. Boris is underestimated by many of his opponents because they can't comprehend his popular, cross-party appeal.

Boris has been dubbed the coalition's worst critic. He lambasted the government's housing policy as 'social cleansing', went against Conservative policy and called for a referendum on the EU, and warned the government to rethink cuts to police numbers in the wake of the London riots. Boris is the darling of the Conservative grassroots and is seen by many as the only man standing up for Conservative values. As I write, he is perhaps the most powerful Conservative politician in the country. But few believe his denials of interest in the top job – that of Prime Minister. Could he one day grab the keys to Number 10? With Boris, you learn to never rule anything out.

I'd like to thank my assistant, Grant Tucker, for his help in compiling this book. Boris has had a deep effect on Grant. He is now sporting a Boris style haircut...

Iain Dale
Tunbridge Wells, August 2011

BORIS FACTFILE

Boris Johnson is a Eurosceptic, British right-wing journalist and former Conservative Member of Parliament for Henley. On 2 May 2008 he was elected as the first Conservative Mayor of London.

Full Name: Alexander Boris de Pfeffel Johnson
Born: 19 June 1964, New York
Siblings: Leo, Rachel, Jo
Education: Eton, before studying Classics at Balliol
              College, Oxford
Married: Marina Wheeler in 1993
Children: Milo, Theo, Laura, Cassia

Career Timeline:
1964   Alexander Boris de Pfeffel Johnson is born in New York City on the 19 June
1977   Attends Eton College as a King's Scholar
1983   Studies Classics at Balliol College, Oxford
1986   Elected President of the Oxford Union
1987   Trainee reporter for *The Times*
1987   Reporter for the *Wolverhampton Express and Star*
1987   Leader and feature writer at the *Daily Telegraph*
1989   Becomes European Community correspondent for the *Daily Telegraph*
1994   Assistant Editor for the *Daily Telegraph*

1994	Political columnist for *The Spectator* (one year)
1997	Unsuccessful in becoming Member of Parliament for Clwyd South
1999	Becomes Editor of *The Spectator*
2001	Becomes Member of Parliament for Henley-on-Thames
2003	Becomes Vice-Chairman of the Conservative Party
2004	Appointed Shadow Minister for the Arts
2004	Nominated for a BAFTA television award
2004	Sacked as Minister of Arts after allegations of an adulterous affair
2005	Resigns from *The Spectator* editorship to take up position as shadow Minister for Higher Education
2007	Announces candidacy for the Conservative nomination for London Mayor. Resigns his position as shadow Minister for Higher Education
2008	Is elected Mayor of London on the 2 May, beating Labour's Ken Livingstone.

THE WORDS OF BORIS

"This is not a time to think about making substantial cuts in police numbers."
After the London Riots of 2011.

"Rugby is a fantastic way of letting off steam. At the end of a game of rugby, you sit in the changing room with the relief of one who has just survived being beaten up by the secret police."
29 March 2011.

"[I am] a wise guy playing the fool to win."
***Sunday Times*, 16 July 2000.**

"We either unleash a full-hearted attack on the nanny-ing, mollycoddling, Harriet Harperson hopelessness of our times, or else too many of our children will grow up fat, unhappy, or violent; we will never win Wimbledon, and football will remain a game in which, in Gary Lineker's immortal words, twenty-two men run around for ninety minutes and then the Germans win."

Daily Telegraph, 1 July 2008.

Boris Johnson: Whatever type of Wall's sausage is contrived by this great experiment, the dominant ingredient has got to be conservatism. *The meat in the sausage has got to be Conservative*, I would say. With plenty of bread and other bits and pieces.

Jeremy Paxman: The question is whether it's a chipolata or a Cumberland sausage, I suppose, is it?

Johnson: This is fantastic to listen to. Enough of this gastronomic metaphor!

Paxman: You started it!

Johnson: Well, I've had enough of it!

Paxman: Haven't you got a city to run?

Johnson: I have got a city to run and that's exactly the point! The government of London will carry on irrespective of the temporary difficulties in providing a national government. Thank you.

Paxman: Bye bye, Boris!

Boris on the possibility of a coalition after the UK general election, *BBC News*, 7 May 2010.

"For ten years we in the Tory party have become used to Papua New Guinea-style orgies of cannibalism and chief-killing, and so it is with a happy amazement that we watch as the madness engulfs the Labour Party."

After apologising for any offence, Boris said he would be happy to 'add Papua New Guinea to my global itinerary of apology'.

"I forgot that to rely on a train, in Blair's Britain, is to engage in a crapshoot with the devil."
Daily Telegraph, 3 July 2003.

"A horse is a safer bet than the trains."
Daily Telegraph, 3 July 2003.

"The dreadful truth is that when people come to see their MP, they have run out of better ideas."
Daily Telegraph, 18 September 2003.

"Spending an hour with the FT is like being trapped in a room with assorted members of a millennialist suicide cult. If their pundits are to be believed, the skies of the City will shortly be dark with falling bankers, and then for the rest of us it's back to the 1930s, with barrels for trousers, soup kitchens and buddy can you spare a dime."

Daily Telegraph, 14 October 2011.

"I rubbed my eyes and emitted a sigh as tragic as Prince Charles on beholding the blueprints for the gherkin."
Daily Telegraph, 15 July 2008.

"Tesco, the destroyer of the old-fashioned high street, Tesco the slayer of small shops, Tesco through whose air-conditioned portals we are all sucked like chaff, as though hypnotised by some Moonie spell."
Daily Telegraph, 15 July 2008.

"Nor do I propose to defend the right to talk on a mobile while driving a car, though I don't believe that is necessarily any more dangerous than the many other risky things that people do with their free hands while driving — nose-picking, reading the paper, studying the A–Z, beating the children, and so on."

1 August 2002.

"I object furiously to the element of compulsion, not just because it offends the principles of liberty, but because the whole problem of politics over the past thirty years is that we have proceeded by central legislation rather than leaving decisions to individuals and to communities."

Daily Telegraph, 20 February 2011.

"I have been asked to have a go in it myself but I think it would be electorally inadvisable."
On the new Olympic pool.

"You're an apple short of a picnic."
On Labour's John Biggs.

"Mr Blobby and Beethoven are yokemates of broadcasting destiny."
16 September 2008.

"We need to remember that we can't compete end-lessly with other nations that set their income taxes substantially lower than ours. They will attract jobs, and investment. They may generate more tax – and they may even persuade their tennis champs to run that extra half yard."
4 July 2011.

"Women cannot resist men who obviously like women."

"A good dry run for the Olympics."
On the Royal Wedding.

"Vote Johnson, vote often – there is a ready supply of Johnsons waiting to step into whatever breaches are left in whatever constituencies."
Boris while out visiting his dad's Teignbridge constituency.

"I will never vote to ban hunting. It is a piece of spite that has nothing to do with animal welfare, and everything to do with Blair's manipulation of rank-and-file Labour chippiness and class hatred."
Friends, Voters, Countrymen

"My chances of being PM are about as good as the chances of finding Elvis on Mars, or my being reincarnated as an olive."

"Life isn't like coursework, baby. It's one damn essay crisis after another."
In an article titled 'Exams work because they're scary', *Daily Telegraph,* **12 May 2005.**

"It is a wonder that the Dutch look so tall and healthy, when you consider what they eat."
Lend Me Your Ears

"I think I was once given cocaine but I sneezed so it didn't go up my nose. In fact, it may have been icing sugar."
Evening Standard, **17 October 2005.**

"I love the skyline of New York, the city of my birth. There are few things more beautiful than the skyscrapers against the cold, bright blue sky. That skyline has now been changed by terror.

But buildings will rise on that site again; perhaps not as big as what was there before; perhaps, knowing the Americans, bigger. That is as it should be. To accept that the world is reshaped is to do the terrorists' work."

"My friends, as I have discovered myself, there are no disasters, only opportunities. And, indeed, opportunities for fresh disasters."
On being sacked from the Tory front bench, *Daily Telegraph*, 2 December 2004.

"If there is one thing wrong with us all these days, it is that we are so mollycoddled, airbagged and swaddled with regulations and protections that we have lost any proper understanding of risk. As long as tobacco is legal, people should be free to balance the pleasures and dangers themselves."
***Daily Telegraph*, 23 June 2005.**

"But here's old Ken – he's been crass, he's been insensitive and thuggish and brutal in his language – but I don't think actually, if you read what he said, although it was extraordinary and rude, I don't think he was actually anti-Semitic."
***The Times*, 17 February 2005.**

"I'm very attracted to it. I may be diverting from Tory party policy here, but I don't care."
On 24-hour drinking legislation.

"Will I throw my hat into the ring? It depends on what kind of ring it is and what kind of hat I have in my hand."
When asked by the *Oxford Mail* if he will stand for leader of the Conservative Party.

"The proposed ban on incitement to 'religious hatred' makes no sense unless it involves a ban on the Koran itself."
***Daily Telegraph*, 21 July 2005.**

"When is Little Britain going to do a sketch, starring Matt Lucas as one of the virgins? Islam will only be truly acculturated to our way of life when you can expect a Bradford audience to roll in the aisles at Monty Python's Life of Mohammed."

"That's one for the memoirs."

Boris after he was rescued after being swept out to sea while swimming.

"Tremendous, little short of superb. On cracking form."
Asked how he was feeling after being sacked as shadow Arts Minister for having misled Michael Howard.

"Nothing excites compassion, in friend and foe alike, as much as the sight of you ker-splonked on the tarmac with your propeller buried six feet under."
On being sacked from the Tory frontbench, *Daily Telegraph*, **2 December 2004.**

"I'm making absolutely no comment … and no, I did not."
When asked if he intentionally misled Michael Howard, leader of the Conservative Party.

"Some time before the end of August, I will grab a week's leave, like a half-starved sealion snatching an airborne mackerel, and whatever happens that leave will not be taken in some boarding-house in Eastbourne. It will not take place in Cornwall or Scotland or the Norfolk Broads. I say stuff Skegness. I say bugger Bognor. I am going to take a holiday abroad."

Boris refuses to take a holiday in Britain.

"It was not only a joy to take the hospitality of the Royal Box. It was a civic duty."
On his decision to watch the Wimbledon final from the Royal Box.

"We need to end the appalling tendency of the present Livingstone regime in City Hall to treat fare-dodging as a kind of glorious Che Guevara two-fingers to the capitalist conspiracy."
On fare-dodging under Ken Livingstone.

"One moment he might be holding forth to a great perspiring tent at Hay-on-Wye. The next moment, click, some embarrassed member of the Welsh constabulary could walk on stage, place some handcuffs on the former leader of the Free World, and take him away to be charged. Of course, we are told this scenario is unlikely. Dubya is the former leader of a friendly power, with whom this country is determined to have good relations. But that is what torture-authorising Augusto Pinochet thought. And unlike Pinochet, Mr Bush is making no bones about what he has done."

Boris warns that George W. Bush could be arrested if he visits the UK.

"I'm a rugby player, really, and I knew I was going to get to him, and when he was about two yards away I just put my head down. There was no malice. I was going for the ball with my head, which I understand is a legitimate move in soccer."

On his tackle on German midfielder Maurizio Gaudino in a charity football match, May 2006.

"Hypocrisy is at the heart of our national character — without the oil of hypocrisy, the machinery of convention would simply explode."

Daily Telegraph, 15 July 2008.

"Let me tell you, if they want a cut-price deal for a central London venue with a view of London landmarks, the ideal place would be City Hall."

Offering City Hall as a cheap venue for the Royal Wedding.

"We can rebuild every part of the city that has been damaged; we can repair every shop; we can make sure that everyone understands the compensation to which they are entitled."

Boris staying resilient after the London riots.

"I am far too terrified to dissent from the growing world creed of global warming."

"Give that man a handbag! And while you're at it, tell him to wear a powder blue suit and a pineapple coloured wig next time he wants to impersonate this century's greatest peace time Prime Minister."
Lend Me Your Ears

"Mrs Thatcher pioneered a revolution that was imitated in one way or another around the world."
Lend Me Your Ears

"It [the 'Building and Buildings, England and Wales' regulation] is the 4,633rd regulation the government has introduced this year. If this government has any architectural legacy whatsoever, apart from the Dome, it will be a host of yawning unrepaired windows. It is through one of those apertures that they should chuck these and other regulations, before it is too late."

"There are not many Lib Dems in Parliament, but even in that tiny group they incarnate dozens of diametrically opposing positions. You want to know what the Lib Dem policy is on taxation, for instance, and you want to know whether you are for or against a 50 per cent tax rate. One half of your cerebrum thinks it quite right that the rich should pay more; the other lobe thinks tax is quite high enough already. You are a perfect Lib Dem, a mass of contradictions, and your party supplies exactly what you are looking for."
Have I Got Views For You

"I'm in charge here!"

When things on *Have I Got News For You* threatened to get out of hand.

"My ambition silicon chip has been programmed to try to scramble up this ladder, so I do feel a kind of sense that I have got to."
Describing his political ambitions, November 2005.

"Hello, I'm your MP. Actually I'm not. I'm your candidate. Gosh."
Canvassing in Henley, 2005.

"It is often immigrants who like waving flags and receiving CBEs, and they certainly seem pretty good at cricket."
Discussing the pros and cons of British immigration.

"If the fuel strikers had not struck, people would never have grasped so clearly how much money Gordon is filching. It is thanks to the fuel protesters that we understand what a regressive tax it is, and how it has helped the tax burden of the poorest fifth of society to rise by three per cent since 1997. It is thanks to the fuel strikers that tax and public spending are now again at the centre of politics. Blair will say he can't cut taxes because it is inflationary, or because he needs to spend the money on pensions, or schools or hospitals. He can't have it both ways."

"All politicians in the end are like crazed wasps in a jam jar, each individually convinced that they are going to make it."
On his political ambitions, November 2005.

"I've got my fingers in several dykes."
Conservative Party Conference, 6 October 2004.

"Their policy on cake is pro-having it and pro-eating it."
Discussing Liberal Democrat policies.

The President is a cross-eyed Texan warmonger, unelected, inarticulate, who epitomises the arrogance of American foreign policy.

On George W. Bush.

"She [Polly Toynbee] in-carnates all the nannying, high-taxing, high-spend-ing, schoolmarminess of Blair's Britain. She is the defender and friend of ev-eryone whose non-job has ever been advertised in *The Guardian* appointments page, every gay and lesbian outreach worker, every clip-board-toter and pen-pusher and form-filler whose func-tion has been generated by mindless regulation. Polly is the high priestess of our paranoid, mollycoddled, risk-averse, airbagged, booster-seated culture of political correctness and 'elf 'n' safety fascism."

Daily Telegraph, 23 November, 2006.

"Ok, I said to myself as I sighted the bird down the end of the gun. This time, my fine feathered friend, there is no escape."
Friends, Voters, Countrymen

"Howard is a dynamic performer on many levels. There you are. He sent me to Liverpool. Marvellous place. Howard was the most effective Home Secretary since Peel. Hang on, was Peel Home Secretary?"
On Michael Howard, *The Times*, 19 April 2005.

"I advise you all very strongly – go for a run, get some exercise and have a beautiful day."

Cornered by reporters asking about his affair after a morning run, 15 November 2004.

"When I look at the streets of London I see a future for the planet, a model of co-operation and harmony between races and religions, in which barriers are broken down by tolerance, humour and respect – without giving way either to bigotry, or the petty balkanisation of the Race Relations industry."

July 2007.

"There seems no reason to behave respectfully towards that little old woman coming out of the Post Office if you feel that she belongs to a culture that is alien from your own... Why not piss against the wall if you feel that it is not really your wall, but part of a foreign country."

Lend Me Your Ears

"I'm kicking off my diet with a cheeseburger – whatever Jamie Oliver says, McDonald's are incredibly nutritious and, as far as I can tell, crammed full of vital nutrients and rigid with goodness."

While campaigning at McDonald's in Botley, Oxford, May 2005.

"The Lib Dems are not just empty. They are a void within a vacuum surrounded by a vast inanition."
On the Liberal Democrats.

"What's my view on drugs? I've forgotten my view on drugs."
During the campaign trail of the 2005 general election.

"Voting Tory will cause your wife to have bigger breasts and increase your chances of owning a BMW M3."

"I didn't see it, but it sounds barbaric. It's become like cock-fighting: poor dumb brutes being set upon each other by conniving television producers."
On *Big Brother*, *The Observer*, 20 June 2004.

"Try as I might, I could not look at an overhead pro-jection of a growth profit matrix and stay conscious."
Explaining why he quit after a week as a manage-ment consultant.

"There is one measurement I hesitate to mention, since the last time I did, I am told, the wife of the editor of *The Economist* cancelled her subscription to the *Daily Telegraph* in protest at my crass sexism. It is what is called the Tottometer, the Geiger counter that detects good-looking women. In 1997, I reported these were to be found in numbers at the Labour conference. Now – and this is not merely my own opinion – the Tories are fighting back in a big way."

The Spectator, 10 February 2001.

"The other day I was giving a pretty feeble speech when it went off the cliff and became truly abysmal. It was at some kind of founder's dinner for a university and I had badly miscalculated my audience. I thought it was going to be a bunch of students, and when I saw the elite group of retired generals, former *Telegraph* editors and Nobel Prize-winning economists, all in black tie, with their wives, I desperately tried to extemporise something profound. There were some musty sepulchres set into the wall of the ancient hall, so I started burbling about social mobility in the eighteenth century and widening participation in universities today. Frankly, I thought, my sermon was more or less ideal. I began some guff-filled sentence with the words, 'I am sure we all agree...' It seemed to go well, so I did it again. 'I am sure we all agree we need world-class skills...', I said, or something equally banal, at which point a man down the table shot to his feet and shouted, 'Well, I don't! I don't agree with what you are saying at all. It seems to me to be quite wrong for you to claim that we all agree when I don't agree.' And blow me down, he appeared to be wearing long purple vestments. It was, of course, Britain's most turbulent priest, the Bishop of Southwark. I realised I was being heckled by a blooming bishop, and from that moment on my speech was irretrievable. I told a long and rambling story about sheep, in the hope that the man of God would be appeased, and sat down. I did sniff him later on, and though there was an aroma of hot cassock he didn't seem notably drunk."

The Spectator, 27 January 2007.

"Yes, cannabis is dangerous, but no more than other perfectly legal drugs. It's time for a rethink, and the Tory party – the funkiest, most jiving party on Earth – is where it's happening."
Daily Telegraph, 12 July 2001.

"I don't see why people are so snooty about Channel 5. It has some respectable documentaries about the Second World War. It also devotes considerable air-time to investigations into lap dancing, and other related and vital subjects."
Daily Telegraph, 14 March 2002.

"We are confident in our story and will be fighting this all the way. I am very sorry that Alastair Campbell has taken this decision but I can see that he got his tits in the wringer."
On Alastair Campbell's negative reply to *The Spectator*'s report that the government had influenced the Queen Mother's funeral arrangements.

"I seemed to be averaging a speed of X and then the M3 opened up before me, a long quiet Bonneville flat stretch, and I am afraid it was as though the whole county of Hampshire was lying back and opening her well-bred legs to be ravished by the Italian stallion."
On driving a Ferrari.

"We can be as nice as pie, we can take our ties off and breakdance down the esplanade and all wear earrings and all the rest of it. It won't make any difference to the electorate if they don't think we're going to offer a new and improved, basically Conservative approach to government."

Conservative Conference, 2005.

"As snow-jobs go, this beats the Himalayas... It is just flipping unbelievable. He is a mixture of Harry Houdini and a greased piglet. He is barely human in his elusiveness. Nailing Blair is like trying to pin jelly to a wall."
Reaction to the Hutton Report, *Daily Telegraph*, 29 January 2004.

"Alan Clark... Here was a man, just like the readers of *GQ, Esquire, Loaded* – all the reassurance-craving magazines that have sprouted in the last ten years – who was endlessly fascinated by the various advantages and disappointments of his own gonads."

"Some readers will no doubt say that a devil is inside me; and though my faith is a bit like Magic FM in the Chilterns, in that the signal comes and goes, I can only hope that isn't so."
Daily Telegraph, 4 March 2004.

"If Amsterdam or Leningrad vie for the title of Venice of the North, then Venice – what compliment is high enough? Venice, with all her civilisation and ancient beauty, Venice with her addiction to curious aquatic means of transport, yes, my friends, Venice is the Henley of the South."
Daily Telegraph, 11 March 2004.

"All the warning we had was a crackling of the alder branches that bend over the Exe, and the stag was upon us. I can see it now, stepping high in the water, eyes rolling, tongue protruding, foaming, antlers streaming bracken and leaves like the hat of some demented old woman, and behind it the sexual, high pitched yipping of the dogs. You never saw such a piteous or terrible sight..."

"[I have been propelled] as a fat German tourist may be transported by superior alpinists to the summit of Everest."
Praising colleagues at *The Spectator* in his leaving speech, December 2005.

"Look the point is ... er, what is the point? It is a tough job but somebody has got to do it."

On being appointed shadow Arts Minister, 7 May 2004.

"It is not just that I love skiing... [I] am more or less addicted to the joy of hurling myself down the slopes."

Daily Telegraph, 20 February 2011.

"I want now to reassure all smokers that in one way I am on their side. It is precisely my continued failure to take up smoking that leads me to oppose a ban on smoking in public places... Above all, a ban on smoking in public places substitutes the discretion of the state for the individual will, in a way that is morally sapping."

She was blonde. She was beautiful. She was driving some poxy little Citroen or Peugeot thing... And she had just overtaken me... And let me tell you, I wasn't having it. Because if there is one thing calculated to make the testosterone slosh in your ears like the echoing sea and the red mist of war descend over your eyes, it's being treated as though you were an old woman by a young woman ... the whole endocrine orchestra said: 'Go. Take.' You can't be dissed by some blonde in a 305.

On driving an Alfa Romeo.

"I'd want to get Blair and really interrogate the guy. I'd really want to pin him up against a palm tree and slap him around and get the truth out of him about a few things we need a bit of elucidation."

"Ken [Livingstone] doesn't think he's got anything to say sorry for and if that's really his feeling, then I think that he should stick to his guns."

"What we hate, what we fear, is being ignored."
On the fears of MPs, 21 April 2005.

"I think they get a fair squeeze of the sauce bottle."
Questioned by Michael Crick on his dedication to his political career and the Conservative Party, 2005.

"It is utterly absurd that Labour should be calling on us all to remember the value of that inclusive word 'British', when it is the government's own devolution programme which has fomented the rising sense of Scottishness and Englishness."
Lend Me Your Ears

"We will demonstrate that we are the party that cares about the older generation by propelling a man who is so full of vim he will give me a thrashing on the squash court and has nine-and-a-half grandchildren."
Trying to get his dad elected in Teignbridge, 2005.

"I'm having Sunday lunch with my family. I'm vigorously campaigning, inculcating my children in the benefits of a Tory government."

Asked whether he was canvassing at Sunday lunch-time, *The Guardian*, 11 April 2005.

"There may be a reason I can't think of but the problem with that reason is that I can't think of it now."

"I have founded the Pie Liberation Front. Our campaign to smuggle traditional British food to schoolchildren begins next week. Will you be our honorary patron?"

"If this is war, let's win it. Let's fly with whatever it takes to the mountain eyrie of Bin Laden, winkle him out, and put him on trial. If we can find good evidence that he is guilty, and he puts up any resistance, then let's not even bother with the judicial process. Let's find the scum who did this and wipe them off the face of the Earth."

"We should be careful, in the current climate, of rushing through legislation that goes too far in expanding the powers of the state. We should beware of eroding our freedoms, when freedom is what we are supposed to be fighting for. O Crime, what liberties are removed in thy name."

"All those snooty Europhile politicians and journalists who sneered at us for our doubts should be forced to crawl in penitence to Dublin Castle, scourging themselves with copies of the Maastricht Treaty. We have been vindicated, and the least they can do is admit it."
Daily Telegraph, **13 December 2010.**

"I've always known my life would be turned into a farce. I'm just glad it's been entrusted to two such distinguished men of letters."

"Och aye, it's the New Jerusalem! It's a land of milk and honey they're building up there in Scotland, laddie. They'll nae be doing with your horrid Anglo-Saxon devil-take-the-hindmost approach. No, they're just more socialist than us sour-mouthed Sassenachs."

"It's economically illiterate. A degree in classics or philosophy can be as valuable as anything else."

"No one obeys the speed limit except a motorised rickshaw."
Daily Telegraph, 12 July 2001.

"The trouble with campaigning in the wilds of Oxfordshire is that you lose touch with the main battle. I feel lost in the jungle, way up the Nong River, seventy-five clicks beyond the Do Long bridge."

"I have not had an affair with Petronella. It is complete balderdash. It is an inverted pyramid of piffle. It is all completely untrue and ludicrous conjecture. I am amazed people can write this drivel."

Denying accusations of his having an affair with Petronella Wyatt, *Mail on Sunday*, 7 November 2004.

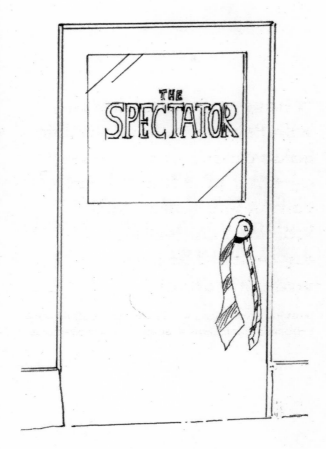

"I got to page 1,264 of *War and Peace*. It was really hotting up, but unfortunately I lost my copy."

"Devolution is causing all the strains that its opponents predicted, and in allowing the Scots to make their own laws, while free-riding on English taxpayers, it is simply unjust. The time will come when the Scots will discover that their personal care for the elderly is too expensive, and they will come, cap in hand to Uncle Sugar in London. And when they do, I propose that we tell them to hop it."

"Here we are in one of the most depressed downs in southern England, a place that is arguably too full of drugs, obesity, underachievement and Labour MPs."
GQ, **2007.**

"It's time they were ejected into outer space."

On the Labour Party, 2005.

"What I would advise fans is to expect little and possibly they'll receive even less."
Commenting on England vs Germany Legends match, 3rd May 2006.

"There is no finer subject. I say that without prejudice to other subjects, which you can basically read in your bath."
On the subject of classics, 2005.

"Statistically, I am due to be fired again."
When asked if he was due to be included in the latest Tory reshuffle, June 2007.

"Celebrating. I do think there's every chance. There's a swing on."
When asked what he will be doing the day after the election, 2005.

"First-past-the-post has served this country well, and served dozens of other countries well. We would be mad to go to a great deal of trouble and expense to adopt a system that is less fair than the one we have."
Boris on the Alternative Vote.

"We are going to have carnivorous festivals of chops and sausages and burgers and chitterlings and chine and offal, and the fat will run down our chins, and the dripping will blaze on the charcoal, and the smoky vapours will rise to the heavens. We will call these meat feasts Pachauri days, in satirical homage to the tofu-chomping UN man who told the human race to go veggie."

After Dr Rajenda Pachauri, Chair of the Intergovern-mental Panel on Climate Change, suggested people should give up meat to stop global warming.

"The whole point about representative democracy is not that it is perfectly representative of the views of the people, but that the representatives should do their duty by their consciences."

"It may be that the psychological effort needed to haul myself around into a more gaffe-free zone proves too difficult."
When asked if he was due to be included in the latest Tory reshuffle, June 2007.

"By all means let us have a referendum – the one we were promised, on the Lisbon EU Treaty."
28 February 2011.

"I have successfully ridden two horses for quite a long time. But I have to admit there have been moments when the distance between the two horses has grown terrifyingly wide, and I did momentarily come off."

Boris reflecting on his very public 2004 downfall, November 2005.

"We are tiny blobs of flesh and blood crawling on the thin integument of a sphere of boiling rock and metal."

Boris on the human race.

"Terrible outbreak of afternoon kipping in Henley. Always in their dressing gowns, hard at it."

"Among the many reasons for mourning the passing of Auberon Waugh is that he will not be here to witness the final obliteration of hunting by the Labour Party... If I were not a Tory, I think I would become one on this issue alone."
Daily Telegraph, 18 January 2001.

"You great big quivering gelatinous invertebrate jelly of indecision, you marched your troops up to the top of the hill in October of [2007]. Show us that you've got enough guts to have an election June 4. Gordon: Man or Mouse?!"
Boris enticing Gordon Brown to call an election for June 2009. Wall Street Journal, 3 January 2009.

"It is time for concerted cultural imperialism. They are wrong about women. We are right. We can't have them blowing us up. The deluded fanatics must be helped to a more generous understanding of the world. Female education is the answer to the global population problem. It is the ultimate answer to the problem of Islamic fundamentalist terrorism."

"The royal family are living memorials, the history of the country written in their DNA, a bit like the inscriptions on the Menin Gate. Unlike the Menin Gate, thanks to human reproduction, those genes can go on for ever."

"I love tennis with a passion. I challenged Boris Becker to a match once and he said he was up for it but he never called back. I bet I could make him run around."

The Express, 21 March 2005.

"They are a bunch of euro-loving road-hump fetishists who are attempting, like some defective vacuum cleaner, to suck and blow at the same time."
Boris on the Lib Dems, *Daily Telegraph*, 19 April 2010.

"My hair has yet to induce epilepsy and cost considerably less than £400,000 to design."
When Boris's hair was compared to the new London 2012 Olympic logo, 9 June 2007.

"Ich bin ein Frankfurter."
Uttered while discussing educational freedom (derived from Felix Frankfurter).

"We are still the second most important country on Earth. The trick of maintaining such influence, of course, is to go around pretending to be very bumbling and hopeless and self-deprecating, a skill at which we excel."

"Reward them for what? You might as well give Lord Cardigan a bonus for the Charge of the Light Brigade."
On bankers' bonuses.

"I'm backing David Cameron's campaign out of pure, cynical self-interest."

On the 2005 Conservative leadership contest, *The Independent*, 5 October 2005.

"Now, there will be plenty of British Conservatives who think these Taliban chappies run a tight ship, women's lib is not an unalloyed blessing, look at all these poofters these days, and so on. There are even ex-feminists, such as Germaine Greer, who will take a perverse pleasure in announcing that women can look very beautiful in a veil."

"I'm like a greased panther, a coiled spring, all that suppressed kinetic energy."
Commenting on England vs Germany Legends match, 3 May 2006.

"Maybe the Tories would do better, and be in a position to act Right, if they began by talking Left, by explaining the minimal Tory view of the state and society. Because no one looking at the Thatcherites' spending record could be in any doubt: those people thought there was such a thing as society."

"One man's Mickey Mouse course is another man's literae humaniores."
Discussing the 'lite' courses studied at British universities.

"That is the best case for Bush; that, among other things, he liberated Iraq. It is good enough for me."
Daily Telegraph, **26 February 2004.**

"I have as much chance of becoming Prime Minister as of being decapitated by a frisbee or of finding Elvis."

Daily Mail, 22 July 2003.

"You know, whenever George Dubya Bush appears on television, with his buzzard squint and his Ronald Reagan side-nod, I find a cheer rising irresistibly in my throat. Yo, Bush baby, I find myself saying, squashing my beer can like some crazed red-neck. You tell 'em boy. Just you tell all those pointy-headed liberals where to get off."

Lend me Your Ears

"This is the government that promised to build a 'New Britain', that told us that 'things could only get better', and what was their salient commitment to the nation yesterday, apart from some hoary old bilge about drunken yobbery? It was to pick on a small group of a few thousand eccentrics who like to potter around the countryside on their horses, endlessly breaking their collarbones, and to tell them that whatever they're doing, they mustn't. This is government of the fox, for the fox, by the fox."

"We're not Hobbits. I am not about building homes for Hobbits."
Boris on the average floor space in London homes, November 2008.

"It is impossible not to suffer a little frisson of fear about what may be beyond those hairy lips. You cannot help speculating about the slavering canine chops that may be right there, about to close over your intrusive politician's fingers."

On his fear of leafleting.

"We need an alternative, and one that doesn't just involve crucifying our landscape with wind farms which, even when they are in motion, would barely pull the skin off a rice pudding."
Have I Got Views For You

"There is no need here to rehearse the steps of matricide. Howe pounced, Heseltine did his stuff. After it was all over, my wife, Marina, claimed she came upon me, stumbling down a street in Brussels, tears in my eyes, and claiming that it was as if some-one had shot Nanny."
Lend Me Your Ears

"We seem to have forgotten that societies need rich people, even sickeningly rich people, and not just to provide jobs for those who clean swimming pools and resurface tennis courts."
Lend Me Your Ears

"When you see a mugging on Holloway Road, and the villain scarpers into the night, there's no point looking around for a policeman. But in due course the police turn up in a high-powered car, and you are ferried with flashing lights, up and down, up and down – in a macho Starsky and Hutch display that has become utterly banal – while the mugger has melted away."

"'Tee hee,' I said to myself as I took in the ludicrously arrogant Darth Vader-style snout. What was it saying, with the plutocratic sneer of that gleaming grille?

It was saying 'out of my way, small car driven by ordinary person on modest income. Make way for Murano!'"

On test driving a Nissan Murano, *Life in the Fast Lane.*

"There is absolutely no one, apart from yourself, who can prevent you, in the middle of the night, from sneaking down to tidy up the edges of that hunk of cheese at the back of the fridge."

On the dangers of obesity, *Daily Telegraph*, 27 May 2004.

"If we Tories wished to reverse just one year's growth in Whitehall, we would have to sack the equivalent of the entire population of Ilfracombe, the seaside town in Devon!"

"I was at this party in Islington the other day and we were all glugging back the champagne, and suddenly I could resist it no longer. The urge rose within me, as though some genie had seized the diaphragm. 'Hague,' I roared. 'Haguey! Don't you think he's absolutely right to say this stuff about crime? Isn't he spot on?' And their eyes bulged like the very crustaceans on the canapes."

"We should never forget that in asking people to vote for us we are essentially asking to take charge of taxation and spending, and that our prime duty is to bring a new and more sensible – and more Conservative – style of economic management ... the public sector is continuing to expand, and Brown is taking ever more money from the private sector to fund this expansion, and therefore preventing its use in wealth creation or the generation of new jobs."
Have I Got Views For You

"Whatever happens in the world, whatever the catastrophe, we approach it like some vast BBC reporter with an addiction to the first person singular. We just have to put ourselves at the centre of the story."
On the Japanese Tsunami, 14 March 2011.

"I had so massacred Bach that I became one of the first pupils in years to fail grade one piano; and still I persevered, in spite of the gentle whispering campaign mounted by my piano teacher to persuade me to give up."

On his childhood aspiration to play piano.

"A cynic would say that they were all stuck on racial awareness programmes; or deployed in desperate attempts to catch paedophiles in ancient public schools; or lurking in lay-bys in the hope of penalising a motorist; or perhaps preparing for the great moment when they will be able to arrest anyone who allows his dogs to chase rabbits, let alone those who go foxhunting."

On the police.

"You can continue to believe in the NHS as the sole and sufficient provider ... or you can conclude that this is one of the reasons why we have a system which treats the patients as dolts and serfs..."

On the NHS.

"The chief constables originally had good reasons for thinking that it was a waste of manpower to have men in uniform pounding the pavements or cycling through tranquil villages. Their men were likely to stumble across a robbery in progress, on average, once every eight years. What the chiefs forgot is the psychological effect of denuding the streets of coppers. There is a sense of lawlessness around, and insolent impunity. As for those policemen who are still on the beat, they have plenty of excuse for feeling assailed by this government."

"If Gordon Brown is on course to win the election, then Elvis Presley is on course to win *The X Factor* and Shergar to win the Grand National."
On Gordon Brown's chances of winning the general election, 1 March 2010.

"You should not underestimate my militant determination to increase cycling."

New Statesman, 26 February 2010.

"Hunting is crucial to Labour, because it gives some contour to the semolina-like blob of Tony Blair's ideology. For the millions of Labour voters who have been depressed by the government's failures in the public services, it is one of the few overt chances they will get for class warfare; and conversely the quarrel over hunting enables Labour ministers to caricature their opponents as tweed-wearing Waugh-reading defenders of atavism."

"Unlike the current occupant of the White House, he has no difficulty in orally extemporising a series of grammatical English sentences, each containing a main verb."
Endorsing Barack Obama, *Telegraph* column, 21 October 2008.

"Look, I wouldn't trust Harriet Harman's political judgement."
When told that Harriet Harman thought he had won the election for London Mayor, *BBC News*, 2 May 2008.

"Had it been us staging the Games, I don't think we would necessarily have done the switcheroo with the girl with the braces"
When asked whether he had any criticisms of the Beijing Olympic Games, *The Guardian*, 21 August 2008.

"We have the right kind of snow, just the wrong quantity"
Radio 2, 2 February 2009.

"Virtually every single one of our international sports were invented or codified by the British. And I say this respectfully to our Chinese hosts, who have excelled so magnificently at Ping-pong. Ping-pong was invented on the dining tables of England in the nineteenth century and it was called Wiff-waff!"

At the ceremonial passing of the Olympic flag from China to the UK, 2008.

"One of the great things about journalism is that if you are in doubt about what to write there is always space for knocking copy – and the more popular and well-loved the topic of your piece, the more acute the demand for someone who is willing to step up and put the boot in."
18 April 2011.

"Kate Middleton is not only beautiful, but nice and kind and sweet-natured and charming and hellishly discreet."
18 April 2011.

"The two men look vaguely similar; they both appear to believe in the efficacy of Grecian 2000; they both favour long and rambling speeches on socialist economic and political theory, with Col. Gaddafi's efforts perhaps having a slight edge in logic and coherence."

Boris comparing Gordon Brown to Colonel Gaddafi, 28 February 2011.

"What is a gaffe? A gaffe is in the eye of the beholder."

Wall Street Journal, 3 January 2009.

"Get rid of the licence fee and you lose the vast red velvet drapes in the Albert Hall saying BBC Proms; and without the BBC Proms there would have been no frenzied Italian conductor, his spasms barely contained by the polished brass of the stand."
Boris Johnson on the licence fee, 16 September 2008.

"It would be an utter travesty to blame these events on the police. The police did not riot. The police did not loot or recklessly set fire to property. The police did not attack innocent bystanders."
Evening Standard, **9 August 2011.**

"Soft is the perfect way to enjoy French cheese, but not how we should approach punishing criminals."

"I remember there were a lot of teacher strikes just after I finished teacher training college. I actually received a letter from a union asking if I'd like to sign up. I replied, tersely of course, explaining that I certainly would not, that I opposed their strikes and that they could stick their offer ... well, you know."

"I hope and believe that Gaddafi's days are now numbered, and that he will either fall victim to the lead-weighted handkerchief in the bunga-bunga tent or else be issued with a one-way ticket to Venezuela where he can live out his retirement, like other fallen socialists, as a consultant to the regime of Hugo Chavez."
On Gaddafi's future.

"I used to love the idea of playing football, but whenever I found myself on the pitch, it was like one of those awful dreams where your feet are made of lead and will not move while everyone else is quicksilvering past, and with ever greater desperation you scythe the air with your boot, and you either miss the ball altogether or else you connect with the shins of some other player and over he goes and – peep – you are penalised yet again, or even sent off."

"I will greatly miss Alan Johnson, not just because he is a nice guy but also for the satisfaction I used to get when I saw a headline saying 'Johnson in new gaffe' and realised it wasn't me."

"I haven't got a cat's chance in hell of becoming Prime Minister ... but as I've said before, if I was called from my plough to serve in head office, then obviously I would do my best."
On his future career.

"I ploughed repeatedly into the grass. I took out one of the runway lights. I span like a bar of soap on a wet bathroom floor, and my course was so unpredictable, I was informed, that there was some risk to the health and safety of the camera crews."
On his *Top Gear* appearance.

"It is no use the Muslim Council of Great Britain endlessly saying that 'the problem is not Islam', when it is blindingly obvious that in far too many mosques you can find sermons of hate, and literature glorifying 9/11 and vilifying Jews."
***Daily Telegraph*, 14 July 2005.**

"The Tuscan palazzo of Count Girolamo Strozzi where he [Tony Blair] forged one of New Labour's few hard-edged ideological positions: he was pro-sciutto and anti-pasto."

"We have created a multi-cultural society that has many beauties and attractions, but in which too many Britons have absolutely no sense of allegiance to this country or its institutions. It is a cultural calamity that will take decades to reverse and we must begin now with what I call the re-Britannification of Britain."
Boris inventing new words.

"It is a cynical attempt to pander to the many who think the world would be a better place if dangerous folk with dusky skins were just slammed away, and never mind a judicial proceeding."
On the introduction of control orders.

"If you ask me my vision for London, let me say that one of the most important things I want is a city where Jacqui Smith feels safe enough to pop out and buy a kebab — at any time of day or night."

17 February 2008.

OTHERS ON BORIS

"It is better to have a serious man being a buffoon than a buffoon pretending to be a serious man."
Andrew Gilligan, *Evening Standard*.

"For all his taste for comedy, he has done nothing as inherently comic as Mayor Livingstone's risible cultivation of the Venezuelan President, Hugo Chavez. It should be asked: who is the real 'joke candidate' here?"
***The Spectator*, 21 July 2007.**

"He may seem like a lovable buffoon but you know he wouldn't hesitate to line you all up against a wall and have you shot."
Jeremy Hardy on Radio 4.

"What the f*** are you doing here?"
A drug dealer, as Boris burst into the man's house as part of a police raid.

"You are a self-centred, pompous twit. Even your body language on TV is pathetic. Get out of public life. Go and do something in the private sector."
Paul Bigley (brother of murdered hostage, Kenneth Bigley) to Johnson on Radio City in Liverpool, 21 October 2004.

"He's the sort of person who 200 years ago would have died aged thirty leading a cavalry charge into a volcano."

Frankie Boyle on *Mock the Week*.

"A bicycle permanently chained to the railings of Downing Street. A blond head bobbing up and down at Prime Minister's Questions. Visiting world leaders receiving lectures in Latin. If David Cameron, George Osborne and their coalition fail, one leading Conservative can say that his hands were clean. Untouched by the compromises of coalition, Boris Johnson is styling himself as the true Conservative."

Tim Montgomerie imagines life under Prime Minister Boris.

"The Mayor of London is clearly the only senior politician with an ounce of sense."

Nigel Farage on Boris.

Q & A

"How can somebody as fat as you get so many good-looking women to find you attractive?"
Ardal Conyngham, Belfast

"This strikes me as a trap question."

"Have you ever taken illegal drugs? If not, why not?"
Lois Beene, Cardiff

"I have and I want you to know that I inhaled. Then I sneezed."

"Do you ever harbour lustful thoughts about the honourable women members sitting opposite you on the House of Commons benches? If yes, which ones?"
Steve Cant, Hastings

"They are all perfectly lovely in their own ways. I am rather shocked that you should ask."

"The people of Liverpool are a crowd of mawkish whingers. Why did you apologise?"
Jim Bernard, Manchester

"In the course of my inglorious pilgrimage of penitence I tried to distinguish between *The Spectator*'s attack on a general culture of sentimentality and grievance – which I stood by – and some offensive errors of fact about Hillsborough, for which I grovelled."

"You confessed to having had a crush on Polly Toynbee. What is it about Polly that seems to drive Tory boys wild?"
Tom Scarsdale, by e-mail

"Oh Lord. It's just she's so bossy and posh. Is that the right answer?"

"Have the Ancient Romans anything to teach the Tories about power?"
Gabriella Kruse, Bristol

"Yeah – that it's easily lost to the Vandals."

"Who is your historical pin-up, and why?"
Amelia Lancaster, Derby

"Pericles. Look at his funeral speech. Democracy. Freedom. Champion stuff."

"Are education standards slipping in Britain?"
Richard Morris, Luton

"Slipping! How could you even suggest it? Every year, comrades, our children are getting better and better at passing exams! Every year we produce more A*–C grade tractors from the Red Star plant! This year an amazing 43.5 per cent of candidates got an A at maths A-level, and guess what the proportion was forty years ago, when far fewer people took maths A-level? It was only 7 per cent! Now you do the maths. Oh, all right, I'll do it for you. That is a staggering 620 per cent improvement by our young geniuses. Let me enter the usual political guff about how hard everyone has worked, and let me congratulate them on their grades. But if too many CVs read like a man falling off a building then the A is useless as a tool of differentiation, and that is why some universities are calling for a pre-U exam to replace A-levels, and that is why there is increasing interest in the IB. We have all connived in the fiction that our kids are getting brighter, because that conceals the growing gulf in attainment between much of the maintained sector and the grammar schools/independent schools. The result is that the market has, inevitably, asserted itself, and in a way that is socially regressive. Which schools, after all, are going to have the resources to prepare their pupils for these new specialised university entrance exams?"

In an outstanding journalistic coup, *The Telegraph* acquired a copy of Boris's Mayoral application form. As you can imagine, it's not a boring dirge of sycophancy – in the 'Challenges faced' section, he writes:

1. *Trying to help raise four children in inner London.*

   Outcome: Too early to call, but looking promising.

2. *Taking on Blair and Campbell in the battle of Black Rod's Memorandum on the Queen Mother's lying-in-state.*

   Outcome: Total victory.

3. *Negotiating Hyde Park Corner by bicycle.*

   Outcome: Survival.

INTERVIEW

As part of the long running 'In Conversation' series in *Total Politics* magazine, Iain Dale interviewed Boris Johnson in March 2011. This is the full uncut interview with never-before-seen material. Enjoy!

How has the Mayor's job differed from what you may have expected on your first day?
It's infinitely better and more difficult.

Difficult in what way?
Just the complexity of running a big city, but like any job over a period of several years it gets easier after the first year or ... for the first eighteen months it's always pretty tough, but after a while you start to understand how it works, where the bends are, where the joints are and you start to work out how to make things happen. So it's been obviously a pretty steep learning curve for someone who was a ... shadow whatever-I-was in the Tory party...

You've forgotten already.
... and basically a journalist, but it's been incredible fun. I mean, the single most difficult thing we've had to deal with is the impact of the worst recession we've had for fifty years. We've had to work extra hard to try to protect Londoners and to keep things moving, and to keep doing things because

one of the difficulties you face is that people will say 'listen, times are so tight, things are so tough, you should just concentrate on getting the Tube moving, keep the buses going, cut costs, protect people in every possible way'. We've done that – we've cut huge amounts of waste out of the system, we've held fares down as low as we possibly can and we've done a huge amount to give people skills and give people opportunities.

But in the end this is a great city with a great future – you've got to keep projects coming and you've got to keep chucking the ball down the pitch for us all to chase after. And so there are lots of things that we want to do, going forward over the next two, three, four years.

What might you have done differently if the recession hadn't happened? Was there something that you know you would've done that you've not been able to do because of it?
What I would've liked not to have done is delay Crossrail by a year or not to make some of the very considerable savings that we've made in TFL. I mean, it would be wonderful instead of having just two cycle superhighways to have twelve within one big bang so everybody could see it. I would have liked to have done the cycle hire scheme all way out west. You're obliged to cut your suit to your cloth, or whatever the expression is, and that's been tough. There are things that we're going to do that we're having to do with private backing – we're building this enormous moving thing in the Olympic park, it's going to be absolutely fantastic. It's the biggest piece of public art in the history of the country and we have had to get private money to do it.

We're going to put a cable car across the Thames, and we'll put some money towards it but we'll need private backing as well. I would like to have gone ahead – if you look at the big ticket items – I would have liked to have been in a position to fund a big extension to the Croydon Tramlink. We are going to put a lot more trams into Croydon, we'll be greatly expanding that network, but we couldn't do it in a big bang in the way that would've been nice. So, funding has been a real problem.

How frustrating is it when you've got control over a certain amount of the budget but a lot of it comes from central government? There have been well-publicised supposed spats between you and George Osborne. Give us a flavour of those negotiations.
The Mayor of any capital city is always going to have stresses and strains with government, and there's no doubt that I think that there was a long and scratchy period when we were negotiating the TFL budget settlement, and that took an awful lot of doing, and everyone will remember there was a period where people were saying 'Crossrail? Forget it.' But I was told several times by senior Cabinet ministers that Crossrail was just not going to be something the coalition could deliver given the funding constraints they were under. Then I was simultaneously told that we couldn't have the upgrades of the Tube because it was all too tight.

But those two criticisms were nothing compared to the very serious reservations the Treasury had about continuing with support for free travel for older people in London or for young people or all the travel concessions we had, or for maintaining the bus network, which is an expensive business because it's an amazing bus network but it costs money, so I had a huge amount of pressure coming in from all sides saying 'these are luxuries, Crossrail's something that could easily be shelved – no one's even heard of it'. I was told about two years or eighteen months ago, the advice given to me was to stop talking about Crossrail. Just don't mention it, take it off the oar.

Who was saying this?
I can't tell you.

Why? Because you'd have to shoot me? What kind of people?
People in government. The message was 'you're going to create a political problem for yourself', but I thought that was complete madness, because even if you have high-speed rail bringing in huge number of people to mainline stations in London – to Euston, Paddington – you need Crossrail. The Central Line can't possibly cope with that volume of passengers, and so we won that argument and then we had to win the argument about the upgrades.

But how did you win the argument – were you saying 'well, look – I can't win next time if I don't get these things done'?
In politics there's an air war and a ground war in all big budgetary arguments, and you've got to win both. The air war is literally going on the airways and talking about it, the ground war is talking about it and making the business case, and actually to give George and Dave their due they did understand that there is a strong business case for Crossrail. And I think what the Treasury has really got now is that

London is the motor of the economy – London drives this thing. If you starve London of energy and growth potential, what's going to happen to the rest of the country?

But why are you the only politician effectively sticking up for the city of London? You don't hear anybody else saying anything about it at all.
I think we're entering a very weird political climate, and we have been for eight months or two years. We're in danger of becoming as a country really adverse to wealth creation and hostile to wealth creators, no matter whether they're bankers or anybody else. And I have to say that alarms me, and of course I want to see bankers – as I was telling old Paxman last night, just to drop a name – doing their bit, and I want to see a much greater sense and philanthropy or whatever you want to call it. I think it's incredible that you've got the gap between rich and poor opening up now in a way we haven't seen since the Victorian epoch, but what we haven't got that they did have in the Victorian era is that sense of duty on the part of the real titanic figures who are making them money.

In those times people really thought it was disgraceful not to endow schools and hospitals and libraries. I mean, look at Carnegie – the endowments people made in the economy. I'll tell you what's happened – and you won't be able to print all this – what's really gone wrong I think is that in America it's thought acceptable to give and be publicly identified as being generous and a big person on the stage of giving, and I think in Britain we don't like that and we're nervous of it, and I think people that have money are nervous of being seen to give in that way. So you see people who have shedloads of dosh who just go and buy grouse moors or something.

But how can we switch that round? I think you're absolutely right – in America there is this culture of philanthropy which there just isn't here, and I think it's partly because rich people don't like to put their heads above the parapet because they'll get them shot off by the media. In America that doesn't happen.

Yes. I think it's utterly sickening that editors who are on £2.8m a year are continually inciting the media to orgies of hatred to anybody who's earning money in this country, and I think it's mad – we need to have a more generous spirit.

Going on to the Olympics, it's incredible to think it's only a year away now. That is going to dominate the last period of your first term, and yet you could have it all taken away from you and Ken could be cutting the ribbon...

Well, we'll see. I think it'll be a very tough fight but I've no doubt that we can win and I think that we'll have some fantastic things to say about what we've done and of what we will do. If you look back over the last couple of years people say 'ah, it's just a few bicycles on the streets'. Actually, London's a lot safer. The murder rate in London is now the lowest since... I don't know...

1978.

1978, thank you. And that makes a big difference to people and what they feel about their city. Bus crime's actually down. Bus crime, partly because of the alcohol ban, is now down by 25 per cent or 30 per cent compared to when I came in. This makes a difference to people's quality of life – we've put in huge numbers of trees, we're on a massive campaign to electrify vehicles in London and so there's an agenda to put the village back in the city and to create a sense of trust, neighbourliness – improve the quality of life. And in all sorts of ways I think it has been working and I'm very proud of a lot of the things that we've done.

There are endless things you could do to make small improvements to people's lives. You can put the Oyster on the Overground railway network – that is an appreciable convenience... Next year do you know what we're going to do – this is a world exclusive – you will be able to, when you get on a London bus, you won't even need an Oyster anymore. You can get out your Visa card and swipe it like that, and eventually that'll happen on the Tube as well. So these incremental changes and improvements to Londoners' lives we will be driving forward. But then the big picture that I will be selling to people in 2012 is what we intend to do for the city for the next twenty-five years and the really big areas of growth. Vauxhall, Nine Elms, Battersea are going to be studied and we'll be able to use the tax increment financing to build two new Tube stations in that growth area. It's going to be one of the biggest opportunity areas in all the area around Battersea power station, it's going to be absolutely incredible. But the only bigger opportunity area in the whole of Europe was of course the Olympic Park, Stratford – everything going to the east of that, south-east of Stratford. So the story that we are going to be telling is about all we're doing to do to drive investment in that part of London and to transform it. If you think back to what Canary Wharf was like thirty years ago when I was starting in journalism, it was a wasteland.

It's now one of the most successful financial districts in the world. So there are things you can do by energy and application that can make a real difference to people's lives. We will have a very powerful vision for development in east London and accompanied not just by a cable car but by a new tunnel under the river to supplement the Blackwall tunnel. I think you've got ... just on London generally, and where we need to be as a city, we've got to be the best place on Earth to live in and to invest in, and I think there are some things we need to start getting right and one of those is clearly the general approach we have to taxation, and I don't think we can endlessly go on with the top rate of tax at 50 per cent.

Well, again, you're the only Conservative that's talking about it...
Well, I don't care. I think it's essential that someone does. Look what's happening to Pfizer – now, maybe it's all to do with some decision, they're pulling out of some particular lines of pharmaceuticals they have been making in the UK. I'm perfectly prepared to accept that explanation. But if you've got very senior executives who've got a choice of living in a jurisdiction with a tax rate of 50 per cent or a jurisdiction with a tax rate of whatever happens to be 35 per cent, I'm afraid these things start to tell. It doesn't happen immediately, it doesn't happen in a...

Do you think it already is happening?
Well, I look at decisions like the Pfizer decision and I am worried. So, get that right. I think we need to set out a vision – a plan for bringing taxation down as the economy grows and indeed using taxation, not

just top rate but also National Insurance – all sorts of ways you can cut taxes to stimulate growth. Look at cutting National Insurance for heaven's sake, get business moving number one. Number two, I think we need to have a plan to deal with the potential for vexatious union activity. I know we'll see ... strikes of the kind that don't have the proper support of their...

But when you were elected you said you'd try to negotiate a no-strike agreement, but there's been no progress on that.
I'm afraid that the unions aren't interested in such an agreement at the moment. I think a more profitable way forward has got to be...

You haven't sat down with them to ask them.
There's got to be ... as soon as I got in I was informed very firmly...

You would've known that before the election that they wouldn't be very keen on it, but if you don't actually talk to them how do you then try and persuade them.
I do talk to them. I talk regularly to the unions. I have a meeting of the south-east region of the TUC.

But when was the last time you spoke to Bob Crow?
Well, as I never tire of saying I am more than happy to... Seriously, the south-east region of the TUC come in so often and we talk about all these issues and I talk to Brendan Barber, but...

But to negotiate a strike agreement you're going to have to negotiate with the individual unions, aren't you?

I've got absolutely no problem about talking with a union that is not in a dispute with TFL and obviously what I won't do is get in and negotiate and pull the rug out from under my negotiators. So, as soon as Bob Crow and the RMT cease to be in dispute about one thing or the other of course I will be more than happy to sit down. There's a great conversation to be had, actually, about all the investment we've secured in the Underground and the way we're going to work together for the benefit of Londoners. But what I do think would be useful would be to help set the context for how we improve the Tube, it would be useful if the government could bring in a threshold so that you didn't have endless strikes triggered by a minority...

And they show no sign of wanting to do that?
Well, my impression is no. My impression is that David Cameron is very keen on it and that matters a great deal.

And isn't the best no-strike agreement to introduce driverless trains all across the network? You'd solve the problem immediately.
Yes. Two days ago I had the huge pleasure of getting on a Jubilee line train and sitting in the cab with a wonderful driver who's a lady of ... you know, she's worked with us for four years and it was inspiring to see how it worked. On the Jubilee line now for the last four weeks we have been running an automated system so basically ... I don't want to minimise what she had to do but all she had to do really was push a button to start, the train moved off and then it stopped automatically, the doors opened automatically, she didn't have to use the brake, no throttle, it was—

There we are, if you lose in 2012, there's a job.
It was inspiring and this is what we will do across the sub-surface lines and eventually across the tube network. The sub-surface lines are the district, circle, metropolitan lines. So technological progress will make a great deal of difference and as we're driving all that forward I don't want to see us being held to ransom by people who want to block progress. Look what we had to do with ticket offices. When you've got the oyster card working so well, it would be completely crazy not to reflect that factor in your arrangements. If you've got people who want to, if the customers want to see staff on the station platform rather than sitting behind ticket offices reading books or whatever then we should help that to happen.

Now just on the Olympic stadium – who is to blame that we were in a situation where it could actually have been demolished immediately afterwards?
It was an absolutely crazy solution. When I came in, I was told 'Sorry buster, you can't have football in this stadium, it's got to be an athletics dustbowl, that's what we've told the IOC and it's got to be athletics and athletics alone.' And I said bollocks to that. I mean, it's an obviously perfect resource for a football club, it would animate the whole area, it would bring jobs, it makes sense with our legacy ambitions, and so...

I suppose the point is that had the football people been brought in from the beginning, we wouldn't be in the situation where one of the bidders was talking about wanting to virtually demolish the whole thing.

QUICK FIRE QUESTIONS

Mayor of London or Prime Minister
Mayor of London! Since it's the best job in the world.

Guilty pleasure?
Painting cheese boxes.

Thing you must hate about yourself
Hotly contested field...[long pause] I suppose I'd love to lose a stone and a half.

Thing you love about yourself
Oh Christ, that really is a hotly disputed area. I don't know. I have a very happy life. I find I'm capable of enjoying almost everything.

Favourite view?
I had the most amazing view of London as I came in from Davos. We circled over the whole city. It's just unbelievable. I realised how utility imposes a pattern on development and how common sense increments to the city produce this absolutely beautiful mosaic of life.

The book you are reading at the moment?
I'm reading about fifteen books at the moment. I've just read Exile *by Denise Mina. The climax is not for the faint-hearted. It will leave you breathless and stunned.*

Favourite film?
Dodgeball *or* The Godfather.

Political hero?
Pericles of Athens.

Political villain?
Alcibiades [Ancient Greek politician, famous for role in the later stages of the Peloponnesian War].

Part of your body you love the most?
My leg you keep pulling.

Frankly, it is stupefying, but I don't want to blame anybody because the Olympics is one of those areas of life where actually people have worked very, very well across parties so I don't want to get into... But it is pretty odd that we got into a position where we're spending nearly half a billion pounds building a stadium with no clear football vocation for it so I did find that mystifying and by the time I arrived at City Hall it was too late to stop that but I think we're going to get to a good solution, one way or another.

Moving onto the election in 2012, do you fear that there's... I mean Gordon Brown effectively, at least in part lost the election for Ken Livingstone, because he was at the height of his unpopularity at that point. Ken Livingstone actually never blamed him much to my surprise. Do you not fear that come 2012 the same thing could happen to you because at that point the coalition's policies are probably going to be at their most unpopular?
Of course. I know this is what the Labour Party is certainly counting on in evicting me on that basis – that's their whole strategy. I think that by 2012, we will have done enough and will have a sufficiently imaginative and exciting programme, we will have done enough to help London's poorest and neediest get through tough times insofar as we've been able to. We've frozen council tax, we've held fares down as far as we possibly can, we've kept the concessions on the buses, we're doing a huge amount to promote apprenticeships for young people, get Londoners through the recession. I think people will understand that we've worked incredibly hard on that and will look ahead and say well do you want

to go forward or do you want to go back? You can go back to the same old politics we had before 2008 or do you want to look at a different vision for London? And I think in the end, although it will be a very tough fight, that argument will prevail.

You won in part because you managed to mobilise the vote in the sort of doughnut as it was described last time, are you going to have a similar strategy this time?
I won Greenwich.

Greenwich is the key. Greenwich is the Basildon of London.
There are plenty of places that I think you know I will fight for, every place and every part of London. I believe we've got a great story to tell about things we've done across the city.

What was the mistake that Ken made last time in fighting you?
Well, fighting me was the mistake [laughter].

He seemed to fire all his ammunition at you from the start, all the sort of racist stuff. You thought, what's he doing this for now, if he's going to do it, do it in the election, and yet he fired all of that sort of stuff right at the beginning and I always think if you're going to paint someone as something there's got to be some little kernel of doubt in people's minds, so they'll think actually, you may be right. But no one seriously thought that you were racist and therefore he failed. Do you think he's going to fight that kind of campaign again?
Well you know...

He's got the same people running it, hasn't he?
Yeah. Probably for my own peace of mind the less I
think about his campaign, and his tactics, the hap-
pier I'll feel. What I want to do is go out and sell what
I think we've done. I love this job, to get back to your
opening question, I think people were in a way quite
surprised to find they'd elected me in 2008.

Why do you think that?
I don't know, there's a sort of mood, people think
crikey, he's—

What have we done?
There's a certain amount of that, but actually I think
on the whole my impression is that we've done a lot
better than people thought we would.

**Well I remember asking Ken Livingstone that ques-
tion – you know, Boris has done a lot better than people thought he would do, and he admitted that yes,
you had done better than he thought you would do.**
Yeah, and I think we've done a lot better than he
would have done actually is the truth. Let's be hon-
est, he made some great contributions to this city,
he really did—

What's the best thing he did?
I can't remember. Well, he developed John Gum-
mer's plan for... You know...

The Oyster card?
Well, that was going to happen anyway, all cities
now have a variant of that, that was good. I think he
was very brave with the congestion charge. It was an
interesting experiment that hasn't really worked. If

you look around the world very few other big cities have imitated it.

Well it's a stealth tax isn't it? It's not a congestion charge. Congestion is back to where it was before.
Well, it was brave but didn't really come off.

Do you not think that if a congestion charge is going to work it's actually got to be pitched at a level that will actually deter people? I mean Jenny Jones [Green Party candidate for Mayor] came out and said that it should be £50 a day, which is clearly barking mad, but she has a point that if it isn't at a high enough level and doesn't deter people it's just seen as a tax.
We did the right thing with the western extension zone and—

Why did that take so long?
The law, my dear Iain, you should try to go through the consultation process... That is one of the things that Ken and I would probably agree on, the delays caused by bureaucracy and consultation procedures is agonising.

But you were elected on a platform of abolishing it. Why couldn't you just say on day one, alright it's gone?
That's actually not strictly true. You mean to abolish the whole thing? What I said was we could consult Londoners about the western zone and so we went through that and we did it and it's gone.

But if you had stood on that platform, you still wouldn't have been able to do it?

That's the tragic truth, even if I had stood on that platform I couldn't have come in and just whipped it out overnight because I would have been judicially reviewed, I'd have been, all the environmental consultations – it just takes forever.

I think that's what puts people off from going into politics now because they think politicians haven't actually got the power any more.
People should go into politics! It's wonderful, I mean look at me. That's rubbish, rubbish, rubbish. You have an amazing opportunity to do things that are beneficial and I don't understand why people don't go into politics. I really don't understand why there was so little competition in the Labour Party to be the candidate, I don't understand it. It was so easy for me.

The Lib Dems haven't even got one.
What's wrong with everybody?

I think because a lot of people felt that the position didn't have enough power.
I've got a bigger budget and more power than virtually the whole Cabinet.

What further powers would you like?
I think the issue in London is the underperformance of schools; I don't want to take over the schools because that has long historical resonances, but I would like a bigger role in schools. I think there's a conversation to be had about how we mobilise young people in London, and the role of City Hall in doing that. We have very regrettable literacy and numeracy rates, still. It has improved, and Andrew

Adonis did a good job when he was running that part of it, with the London challenge, but it's still really, really holding us back as a city.

What about other cross-party things, for example when there was all the snow. I had people on my LBC programme every night saying 'it's Boris's fault'. And yet you haven't got the powers to do anything.
The single biggest power I want is over the railways in the area. People complained about the trains not coming in from south-east London because of the snow, they were blaming me. I think it came up on your show. It's absolutely predictable that they should blame me because they assume I'm in charge of every railway service in London, but I'm not.

We, Transport for London and the mayoral team, need a say in the franchising of these TOCs, because otherwise we can't set the standards, we can't help to determine timetables, we can't ring them up and say, 'Listen, communicate with the public and tell us why you can't get your trains in.' We at London Underground were able to run all our Overground service, why couldn't the TOCs do it?

Why is ambition seen as a bad thing in politics? If anyone actually comes out and said 'I want to be Prime Minister', they get crucified for it.
Do people get crucified for it? I don't think so. Didn't Heseltine have a famous plan to become Prime Minister and all this business?

He did. Whatever happened to him?
I think the reason people don't trumpet their ambitions is that they're afraid they won't succeed, and they will be teased for failing.

But people accuse you of having Heseltinian ambitions.
Well this is all part of a brilliant stunt by the media to torture me. But as everybody who knows Westminster and understands how politics works, I haven't got a cat's chance in hell of becoming Prime Minister, but it's fun to run this argument, and to torment me.

Even if you think there isn't a cat's chance in hell, would you quite like the opportunity were it to arise?
As I've said before, if I was called from my plough to serve in head office, then obviously I would do my best.

Do you miss the House of Commons?
I haven't really missed it that much I have to admit. I love doing what I do.

I was a little surprised when you stood down. I thought it would be great to have the Mayor of London in the House of Commons because it gives you a national platform, but I suppose if you have a constituency outside London it's a bit difficult.
It's so difficult. South Oxfordshire is a different kettle of fish. It wouldn't have worked in the long run.

Can you see yourself back in there at some point?
I think Guto [Hari, his press officer] will be there before I'm there. You'll be there! Do you remember that memorable day when you were a candidate in Norfolk and I came to visit? It is seared on my mind.

I thought I had it all sorted out.
I was completely thrown. I got up and I couldn't remember what was going on that day, and

I got up and this chap appeared at my door from *Time* magazine—

Michael Wolf from *Vanity Fair*.
Vanity Fair that's right. And we had to get to your place in Great Yarmouth or something.

It wasn't Great Yarmouth! It was Norwich you were supposed to get to. You rang me up at ten to ten, you said 'I'm nearly at King's Cross.' I said 'You're supposed to be at Liverpool Street!' I then had to say 'Get on the train to Peterborough'
That was a total mistake.

So I then had to drive right across Norfolk to pick you up in my very small car.
You were heroic.

I had this famous *Vanity Fair* journalist in the back of my car.
Yes and he was getting ever more cocky about...

We went to this glass factory, and then we had lunch and we were an hour and a half late. We walked in to a Conservative Party fund raising launch and I said to you 'We're going to get lynched' and we walked in, and they all stood up and cheered. I thought to myself: 'Only you could get away with this'.
Actually, lunch was very enjoyable. And then what did we do?

Then you went off to Great Yarmouth to visit Mark Fox, the candidate there.
That's it.

And I went home and had a cold shower.
I'm very sorry.

It was great. I'm very grateful.
No matter how bad, I don't think it cost you.

I don't know, I lost by 10,000.
You didn't!

I did. Never again. I'm very happy on LBC.
You do a great job. Why have you given up blogging then?

I just haven't got the time to do it anymore. I used to do it in the evenings, and I obviously can't do that anymore, so it had to go.
Can't they just put out transcripts...?

I don't think that would really work. Let's continue. What do you think Tory MPs think of you, particularly the new lot? Do you mix with them much?
I haven't got the faintest idea. Well, my brother Joseph I know very well.

Oh really?! The bastard beat me for that one.
Oh did he? They all seem incredibly bright. I suppose I know some of them.

But you don't have groups of them in for a drink from time to time.
No, I don't.

People might misconceive that as leadership ambition, I suppose.
No no, what I think we should do, and one thing I

would love to see is, I'd love to raise the conscious-ness of London MPs about some of the things we're doing a bit more. We were trying to do that.

What's the point of the GLA?
The Assembly?

Whenever I see you appearing in front of them for your question time sessions, you do appear to treat them with complete and utter contempt, and I completely agree with you.
Do I?

I think it's a completely useless body, and it's a huge cost to the public purse and performs very little value.
They're there to scrutinise the mayoral team, which is actually a very powerful institution, with a lot of money at its disposal, so they need to invigilate it. On the whole, actually, I think they do quite a good job. They produce some very good reports.

What happens to them?
Well, we take account of them. Sometimes we imple-ment them.

Sometimes.
Sometimes we file them vertically.

Ten per cent of them? Five per cent of them?
I don't know, but they're influential.

But they're bloody useless at asking questions.
They're not individually paid a huge amount of money, as far as I can remember.

They are, they're paid nearly as much as MPs.
Is that right?

Yes, they're paid over fifty thousand.
Uh-huh. Well. You need a scrutiny body and I work with what I've been given. One of the things we're trying to do is rationalise some of the other functions. The LDA, the development agency, we've folded in. The Metropolitan Police Authority we're going to fold in; there's a bit of a reduction in the overall number of bodies.

I've said right from the beginning that you ought to get rid of Peter Hendy, because I think that he continues to implement Ken Livingstone's transport policy and rather pulls the wool over your eyes. But he's still there and Transport for London is still remarkably inefficient, I think.
We're running a huge city and, actually if you look at performance on the Tube, which has been difficult because of the upgrades we've been putting in over the last couple of years, it is now at last starting to improve. It's not just ridership that's going sky-high, with people actually using it, but also at last the passenger miles, and the miles travelled by the trains is going up. Because of the upgrades, we have to close the Jubilee line at weekends to do it up. It's unbelievably frustrating to have to tell people: 'I'm sorry you can't travel at the weekend because we're upgrading the signalling.'

At last we're starting to see some of the benefits. On the Jubilee line you will start to see things pick up. It has taken time and a great deal of effort and money but, of course, people will always blame me or Transport for London.

They do things which seem completely crass to the travelling public like closing the District line on Saturdays when West Ham have a home game and they're not shutting it when they don't.

That does seem crass to me. I'll look into it. We try not to do that.

The Blackwall Tunnel. It's remarkable shutting it 9pm at night. Why not have it like the Rotherhithe Tunnel with two-way traffic. They seem to go out of their way to inconvenience people.

The Blackwall Tunnel is having a massive upgrade with huge amounts of money being put into it. Traffic flow both ways has increased.

Not between 9–5 at night it hasn't...

No... Overall it has increased. One of the things I will do in my second term is begin work on a second tunnel in Silvertown.

Boris Island airport, which I've been a leading proponent of for years; it's not going to happen is it so why not give up?

The position we've got ourselves into at the moment is because we need a new airport, we need more aviation capacity. I think the idea you can go on without any increase in runway space in the south east is completely nuts. Other European countries are adding runways to say nothing of Dubai, Chicago, you name it. Two things are happening, we are shipping jobs in aviation overseas because we are not the great hub we were. Heathrow has slipped down from the top to seventh in Europe and we're not going to be able to send our business people directly to the places they need to be. The statistic I point out to people is Paris and Frankfurt have more flights to mainland China than all London airports. We have five a day from all London airports and that's to Beijing or Shanghai. In Paris they have ten flights a day to four different destinations. Frankfurt has eleven flights to six destinations. If Britain is going to pull itself up by exposure to the great economies of the East, China and India, we need to get there. You can't get there by high-speed rail so we need more aviation capacity.

What you can't do is then cram a quart into a pint pot at Heathrow. A third runway would be unbearable because of the extra air traffic movements (ATMS) over London. You'd have another couple of hundred thousand flights a year; it would hugely erode the quality of life for people in the city. Even if you did have a third runway it wouldn't provide enough capacity. You need a solution. That's where I've got to. Unfortunately business is in a completely false sense of consciousness. All these people in business think it's only a matter of time before the government gives in and builds them a third runway. They're wrong. It's not going to happen. They need to get that idea out of their heads.

We've never been good at vision in this country. These big infrastructure projects. The channel tunnel I guess was the last one. You can say all you like but you don't have the powers to actually do it.
I know. I've got to keep going because I know I'm right. In the end, the arguments for growth and dynamism will succeed. Aviation is one of the things this government, you've got to get tax right, unions right. Send out a very positive message what this country and this city is all about. At the moment, I worry about a negative signal.

THE BORIS BIBLIOGRAPHY

Friends, Voters, Countrymen, HarperCollins, 2001
Lend Me Your Ears, HarperCollins, 2003
Have I Got Views For You, HarperCollins, 2006
Seventy-Two Virgins, HarperCollins, 2004
The Dream of Rome, HarperCollins, 2005
Aspire Ever Higher, Politeia, 2006
Life in the Fast Lane, HarperCollins, 2007
Perils of the Pushy Parents, HarperCollins, 2007
The British, HarperCollins, 2011
Johnson's Life of London, HarperCollins, (Forthcoming)

Boris on the Web
Official Website: www.boris-johnson.com
Boris Watch: www.boriswatch.com
Boris Mayoral Re-election Campaign:
    www.backboris2012.com

By others:
Boris: The Rise of Boris Johnson, Andrew Gimson,
    Pocket Books, 2007
Boris v Ken: How Boris Johnson Won London,
    Giles Edwards and Jonathan Isaby, Politico's
    Publishing, 2008

Twitter:
Boris on Twitter @mayoroflondon

Dishonourable Insults
A cantankerous collection of political invective

Greg Knight

Dishourable Insults features over one hundred years
of political invective and insult. From Churchill
to Cameron, Balfour to Brown, Curzon to Clegg,
Douglas-Home to Duncan Smith, Healey to Howard,
Macaulay to Miliband, Greg Knight has once again
compiled a witty collection of barbed insults and
invective that will provide amusement and a
delightful source of reference for anyone searching
for the ultimate put-down.

Tory MP on David Cameron: 'Never trust
a man with a woman's mouth.'

288pp hardback, £12.99
Coming soon to all good bookshops
www.bitebackpublishing.com

Prime Minister Boris
and other things that never happened

Iain Dale and Duncan Brack

The grand passage of political history is steered by
a combination of events great and small; assessing
how matters might have turned out under different
circumstances is one of the most intriguing – and
entertaining – historical exercises. This book imagines such tantalising political questions as: What
if Nixon had beaten JFK in 1960? What if Arnold
Schwarznegger had been able to run for President?
And, of course, what if Boris Johnson were to
become Prime Minister in 2016?

376pp hardback, £14.99
Coming soon to all good bookshops
www.bitebackpublishing.com

The Yes Minister Miscellany

Antony Jay and Jonathan Lynn

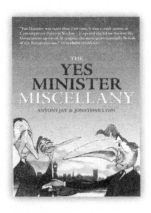

A collection of the funniest sketches, anecdotes, interviews, lists of interesting facts, character and actor profiles, and personal recollections from the enduringly timeless series *Yes Minister* and *Yes Prime Minister* in one perfect small format volume. *Yes Minister*, together with its sequel, *Yes Prime Minister,* is one of the most popular and critically successful British sit-coms of all time, partly due to its fascinatingly accurate observations of the sparring between Paul Eddington's naïve senior minister, Jim Hacker, and Nigel Hawthorne's infernally cunning Permanent Secretary, Sir Humphrey Appleby.

288pp hardback, £6.99
Available in all good bookshops
www.bitebackpublishing.com

You Don't Know Sh*t
The ultimate toilet book

Doug Mayer, Val Stori and Tod von Jahnes

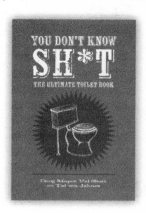

Know your WAG BAG from your honey bucket? Your fecal veneer from your fecal fall-out zone? Laid-back enough to 'go left'? Familiar with the most fart-tastic of bodily functions? With fun facts about everything from the famous Thomas Crapper to the chemicals that make poo smell, as well as the finest diagrams, drawings and could-that-really-be-what-I-think-it-is photos, this encyclopedia of all things scatological guides you from ignorance to expertise in a flash (or flush). So take a seat on your porcelain throne, take your time and read it well, and no one will ever be able to tell you that you don't know your sh*t.

224pp hardback, £9.99
Coming soon to all good bookshops
www.therobsonpress.com

Not In Front of the Corgis
Secrets of life behind the royal curtains

Brian Hoey

In *Not in Front of the Corgis*, veteran royal
commentator and author of more than twenty
books on the royals, Brian Hoey, peeks behind
the curtains to tell us what the royals really get up
to in their spare time. What does the Queen watch
on TV? Why does she not have a driving license?
Who are the most popular royals to work for,
and who the least? Who is the grandest of the
Queen's children and why? *Not in Front of the
Corgis* is a unique and fascinating miscellany
containing everything you ever wanted to know
about the royal family, away from the spotlight.

256pp hardback, £14.99
Coming soon to all good bookshops
www.therobsonpress.com